The Plan

By Robert D. Jones

Chapter One: Miami Heat

Otis didn't trust luck. It wasn't strategy — just a lazy god with bad aim.

It came too easy, left too fast, and usually got you into something a bullet couldn't fix. Still, he leaned hard on it — like tonight, standing at a blackjack table in a smoky casino just off Biscayne Boulevard, with a cocktail in one hand and ten thousand dollars of someone else's money on the felt.

Leon stood behind him, arms crossed, radiating disappointment like heat off a sunburned hood.

"You realize you're gambling with the rest of our trip money, right?"

Otis didn't look up. "Correction: I'm doubling the rest of our trip money."

"Or losing it. Again."

The dealer flipped the next card.

Otis smiled.

Blackjack. The card hit like fate pretending it wasn't rigged.

Leon groaned. "I hate you."

"That's fair."

INT. CASINO FLOOR – LATER

Otis walked like a man who just robbed time — pockets heavier, sunglasses on indoors, humming some 70s soul groove that didn't match the club music rattling the walls.

Leon trailed behind him, counting bills like a grieving accountant.

"Okay, we've got enough for a rental and gas, maybe a motel in Georgia if we skip food."

"Or," Otis said, "we flip it one more time and fly home first class."

"Or," Leon echoed, "we live long enough to tell this story to a therapist."

They cut through the far corridor toward the exit. And that's when Otis felt it.

That tickle.

Like someone had whispered his name just behind his ear.

He paused. Looked back.

Nothing. Just a nun — yes, a nun — walking across the far end of the casino, head down, blending in like smoke.

Her lips were moving. No phone. No prayer.

"You see that?" Otis asked.

Leon turned. "What?"

"Never mind."

EXT. CASINO PARKING LOT – NIGHT

Outside, Miami air clung to skin like bad cologne. The lot was half-lit, half-cracked, half-empty.

Otis spotted a guy in a cheap suit storming toward a black sedan, shouting into a phone. Case in hand. Sweating.

Another man followed at a distance. Calm. Silent.

Otis froze.

There was a flash — not like a gun, something odd that made them pause for just a moment. A misstep. The case clattered to the pavement.

The shouting man got in the sedan and peeled off.

The calm one watched. Then turned and disappeared into the night.

Otis stared at the briefcase.

Leon stared at Otis.

"Don't you even think about it."

"It's just sitting there," Otis said.

"So are bear traps."

But Otis was already moving.

EXT. MOTEL ROOM – LATER THAT NIGHT

They sat on the bed, case between them. Unopened. Heavy.

Leon cracked a beer. Otis just stared at the latches.

"You really don't wonder where this came from?" Leon asked.

Otis shrugged. "We open it, we're involved."

"We already stole it. I think involvement's a done deal."

Otis stared out the motel window, the briefcase between them like an accusation. Something about it gnawed at his instincts, whispering a warning he couldn't quite understand. Whatever this was, it was far bigger than a simple theft. They needed to move, and quickly.

Chapter Two: The Slip

The motel room smelled like bleach, cheap cologne, and anxiety.

Otis paced, tossing a mini shampoo bottle from one hand to the other. Leon sat on the edge of the bed, arms folded, watching the briefcase like it might grow legs and sue them.

"So you're seriously not gonna open it?" Leon asked.

Otis shrugged. "We open it, we're involved."

"We already stole it. I think involvement's a done deal."

Otis glanced at the case. Still closed. Still humming with the weight of something important. Something that didn't belong in a beat-up sedan or a cheap Miami motel.

He turned back to the window. Pulled the curtain aside.

No one there.

But he couldn't shake the itch.

That same feeling from the casino.

Like someone had whispered his name just behind his ear. Something was following them. Watching.

"We need to ditch the road," Otis muttered.

EXT. PARKING LOT – LATER

Leon stuffed their duffel into the trunk of the rental.

"So where we headed? Home, or whatever comes after home?"

Otis popped the trunk and tossed in a snack bag, glancing back at the room like it had tried to keep a secret.

"We lay low. Atlanta maybe. Somewhere nobody's looking."

"Who would even be looking?" Leon asked. "We didn't do anything illegal. I mean—technically."

Otis didn't answer.

Because he'd seen something else on the casino floor. A man in a gray coat. Standing too still. Watching too little.

"I think we're being watched."

Leon sighed. "Of course we are. You keep stealing mystery briefcases like you're on a scavenger hunt hosted by the CIA."

INT. RENTAL CAR – HOURS LATER

The case sat between them like a third passenger.

Otis kept glancing at it.

"It's weird, right? That he just left it."

Leon shook his head. "Not weird. Suspicious. There's a difference. One leads to jokes. The other leads to shallow graves and Wikipedia pages."

"You're really not even a little curious?"

"Nope. You are. That's the difference between us. I let danger walk past. You flirt with it."

Otis grinned. "Danger flirts back."

"And she's probably Clarice, 5'9", armed, and owns a satellite."

They drove in silence.

Then the briefcase beeped.

Just once.

Soft. Electronic.

Otis and Leon locked eyes.

"We open it," Otis said, "we're involved."

Leon nodded.

"You said that already."

Otis reached for the latch.

Otis's hand hovered over the latch, heart hammering. This briefcase, this moment—it felt like stepping off an edge he couldn't see. He glanced at Leon, whose expression mirrored his apprehension. Taking a deep breath, Otis pushed forward into uncertainty.

Chapter Three: The Case

The click of the latch echoed louder than expected.

Otis opened the briefcase slowly, like it might hiss or bite.

Inside?

Not stacks of cash. Not diamonds. Not a severed thumb.

Just...

Paperwork.

Rows of it, labeled and sorted in manila folders with military precision.
A black flash drive, embedded in custom foam.
And a small metal device — smooth, palm-sized, with a fingerprint scanner on top and no logo.
High-end. Government-grade. Something out of a spy movie.

Leon blinked.

"...We risked our lives for tax papers?"

Otis ignored him. He picked up the device and brushed his thumb over the scanner.

It beeped.... Only once.

A green light blinked on.

Leon flinched. "Okay, that felt personal."

Otis stared at the green glow. It hadn't done anything else — no projections, no hidden weapons — but it had reacted to him.

"That doesn't make sense," he muttered.

"What kind of case knows your fingerprint?"

"The kind that was meant for me."

Silence.

The weight of it started to settle in.

INT. GAS STATION – AN HOUR LATER

Leon stood at the window, watching the pump count climb. Otis was inside at a dusty booth, laptop open, device connected through a sketchy adapter he'd borrowed from a teenage cashier who looked like he did freelance hacking while scarfing down hot dogs.

"So what's on it?" Leon asked, sliding back in.

Otis pointed at the screen.

"Encryption. Layered. Some of it military. Some of it... I don't even recognize."

"English?"

"Barely. Most of the file names are redacted."

He clicked one: REMNANTS_001

Denied.

Clicked another: PROJECT_SWITCH

Prompted for biometric access.

Leon rubbed his face. "Let me guess — it wants you again."

Otis hesitated.

"This wasn't just lost. Someone planted it."

Leon stared at him.

"You're saying this was on purpose?"

Otis nodded slowly. "Yeah. I think this is a setup."

"For who?"

"Me."

EXT. HIGHWAY OVERPASS – NIGHT

Far off in the distance, a car sat parked beneath an overpass.

Engine off. Lights off.

A man stood leaning against the hood — motionless, broad-shouldered, face obscured by shadow.

He spoke into a secure line.

"They opened the case."

A pause.

Then: Clarice's voice. Calm. Cold.

"And?"

"It responded to him."

Silence.

Then:

"Good. That means he's ready."

Staring into the darkness from the gas station window, Otis felt an unshakable weight settle on his chest. This wasn't coincidence; it was design. Someone wanted him right here, right now. The question was why—and who would come next.

Chapter Four: Tagged

Otis stared out at the neon-lit streets of Miami, the colors flickering in patterns that seemed almost comforting. But comfort was fleeting, and his mind inevitably drifted back to another night, many years ago, in a smaller house on the outskirts of the city, the sounds of an argument echoing through thin walls.

He was seven years old, sitting on the worn carpet of his bedroom, knees hugged tightly to his chest. His parents' voices rose and fell like storm-driven waves, carrying tension and words he didn't fully understand but felt deeply. Money, trust, responsibility—these fragments of conversations formed the soundtrack of his childhood.

"Trust," his father had said once, sitting Otis down at their delapidated kitchen table, the air heavy with cigarette smoke and unspoken tension. "Trust will get you hurt, kid. You trust yourself first, everyone else second."

That lesson, harsh and clear, became the foundation upon which Otis built his entire identity. His father, despite his constant absences and emotional distance, was an enigma that Otis both feared and admired. He taught Otis card games—blackjack, poker—as if imparting essential life skills. Each game was a lesson in risk assessment, in reading subtle cues, in managing what you reveal and what you hold back. His father's rare approval, marked by a curt nod or a fleeting smile, became a prize Otis sought with a desperation he could never quite conceal.

Yet, those moments of connection were rare stars in an otherwise dark sky. His father's absences, sometimes days, sometimes weeks, left him and his mother struggling to make ends meet, feeding on a diet of uncertainty and insecurity. Otis learned early to mask his fears behind a façade of humor and bravado, becoming adept at deflecting attention from his vulnerabilities.

The fear of abandonment was a quiet yet constant companion, manifesting subtly in his adult relationships, making genuine connection elusive and difficult. He hated feeling vulnerable, despised relying on others, yet he yearned desperately for a sense of belonging.

Now, as he stood overlooking the city where it all began, Otis felt the weight of the past pressing heavily upon him. Project Switch, his father's legacy—discovered by chance or perhaps fate—was a burden that intertwined deeply with his own identity. It was both an opportunity and a curse, a path to understanding the man who shaped him and an ominous threat to the life he'd built so carefully in defiance of that very legacy.

He turned from the window, his reflection fading as he stepped into the dimly lit room. The briefcase lay open on the table, its secrets spilled out in coded files and encrypted drives. He knew it wasn't just about decoding Project Switch; it was about decoding himself—about finally confronting the shadows his father cast over his life.

Otis exhaled slowly, feeling the familiar pull of uncertainty but also a rising sense of determination. He wasn't just his father's son. He was his own man, shaped by hardship but not defined by it. Whatever came next, he would face it on his own terms, driven by the same resilience that had gotten him this far. It was time to face the truths he'd spent a lifetime running from.

Project Switch was never meant to fall into civilian hands. It was a ghost program buried under layers of digital shadows, designed for one purpose: total system control — data, surveillance, communication, infrastructure. Everything.

Otis now stood at the core of it all.

The briefcase was just the beginning — a key, yes, but also a trigger. Activating the contents hadn't just set off a hunt; it had reawakened something buried, something built by his father and hijacked by those who saw the world as code to be rewritten.

Clarice wanted that power. Not to protect anyone. Not to secure peace. But to rebuild the world in her image — efficient, obedient, and monitored. The Tall Man? He was her shadow, a believer in order without mercy. They didn't see Otis as a person. He was a variable. A living access code.

But Otis wasn't just running anymore.

He understood now: this wasn't about finding answers. It was about choosing sides. Either he would dismantle the system his father helped build — or he would become the next ghost in the machine.

Leon, Ava, Trina — they each had a stake, but Otis? He was the axis. Project Switch responded to his biometrics for a reason. His father didn't trust the system, and he didn't trust the people running it. So he embedded his trust in blood — in Otis.

Now, every step forward tightened the grip of those chasing them. Every attempt to uncover the truth buried them deeper in a past that refused to stay dead.

This was no longer about escape.

It was about war.

And Otis was the last firewall.

They didn't notice the tail until Georgia.

The old truck had been behind them for two exits, always two cars back, never passing, never falling away.

Leon adjusted the rearview. "You seeing this?"

Otis nodded. "Yeah."

"That guy's been with us since the state line."

"Could be coincidence."

Leon snorted. "You don't believe in coincidence. You gamble for groceries and talk about gut feelings like they're GPS directions."

Otis cracked the window. Air rushed in. The breeze helped him think. Or pretend he was thinking.

"We need to ditch the road."

EXT. BACK HIGHWAY – NIGHT

They took the next exit. Wound down a county road flanked by trees and signs for towns that probably didn't exist anymore.

The truck followed.

Too close now.

Otis killed the lights and veered off onto a dirt access path.

Leon clutched the dashboard. "Dude—!"

"Better to lose 'em in the dark than get boxed in on asphalt."

They drove half a mile in silence.

Then they parked.

Then they waited.

EXT. WOODS – MOMENTS LATER

Crunching gravel.

Two sets of footsteps.

Not law enforcement.

Not Clarice's kind of quiet either.

This was sloppy confidence — like someone used to winning just by showing up heavy.

Bounty hunters.

Otis whispered, "You armed?"

Leon held up a tire iron. "Only emotionally."

The first man appeared in the clearing — flannel shirt, tactical vest, smile like he practiced it in mirrors.

"Gents," he called, "how about we make this easy?"

"You first," Otis said, stepping out. "Who sent you?"

"Private contract. Real deep pockets. Wants that case. Doesn't care what condition you're in when we deliver."

Leon stepped out too. "See, that's your first mistake."

"Yeah? What's that?"

Leon picked up the tire iron and slowly tapped it into the palm of the other hand. "Thinking we're easy."

FIGHT – QUICK, MESSY, REAL

It wasn't movie clean. It wasn't choreographed.

It was fists, knees, dirt, breath, panic.

Otis took a hit to the ribs and gave back worse.
Leon cracked one guy's jaw with the iron and didn't stop until he stayed down.
They weren't trained — but they were desperate.

And desperate wins fights.

EXT. DIRT ROAD – LATER

Otis wiped blood from his mouth and popped the trunk. The case was still there.

Untouched.

Leon was breathing hard, sitting on the bumper.

"So this is the part where we decide if we're gonna die over this thing, right?"

Otis didn't answer right away.

He looked at the case. Then at the forest. Then at the night.

"This isn't about the case anymore."

Leon looked up.

"Then what is it about?"

Otis stared at the trees.

"Me."

INT. OBSERVATION VAN – UNKNOWN LOCATION

The Tall Man stood alone.

No Clarice. Just shadows.

In his hand, a burner phone buzzed once.

A single text:

"REBOOTING ISN'T DEFEAT. IT'S EVOLUTION." – C

He closed his eyes.

Slipped the phone into his coat.

And walked away.

Otis looked away from the neon-lit streets, his mind racing back to his troubled childhood. Every shadow held memories he'd tried hard to bury. Project Switch wasn't just his father's legacy—it was his own unresolved history demanding to be faced.

Chapter Five: Trina

The bus pulled up with a screech, like the brakes were screaming in protest.

It wasn't a city bus. Or a tour bus. It was a rolling nightclub, wrapped in LED lights and hand-painted flames, with speakers that could be weaponized in three states.

The door swung open.

Trina.

High ponytail. Big sunglasses. Gold hoops. Camouflage crop top and zero regard for the law of volume.

"Get. In."

Leon blinked. "Nope."

Otis was already walking toward the door.

"Otis, come on," Leon hissed. "She's unstable."

"She's reliable because she's unstable," Otis said. "And she owes me."

"For what?"

Otis grinned. "Bail money. 2017. Long story."

INT. PARTY BUS – MOMENTS LATER

Bass thumped. Lights flashed. Somewhere in the back, a fog machine hissed like a malfunctioning dragon.

Trina grinned behind the wheel like she was on something stronger than caffeine and freer than parole.

"You always into something as usual," she said. "But at least you brought the cute one back."
She winked at Leon.

Leon sank into a cracked leather bench. "Please don't flirt while we're fleeing from heavily armed bounty hunters."

"Ohhh, we got drama?" Trina clapped her hands. "Spill it. You got a case? Secret files? Body in the trunk?"

Silence.

Otis didn't answer.

Trina froze for a half second — just a flicker.

"Wait... y'all really got something?"

Otis nodded.

Trina sat back, suddenly serious. Just for a moment.

"Damn. I thought you were just broke and reckless. Turns out you're dangerous too."

EXT. PARTY BUS – ON THE MOVE

They rolled down backroads and county highways, leaving the wreckage in Georgia behind.

Leon rubbed his temples. "This feels like one continuous dream."

"It's only a dream if you wake up," Trina called from the front.

Otis sat by the window, staring out, the case by his side.

"What if someone put this whole thing in our hands on purpose?" he asked.

Leon glanced at him. "They did. We stole it."

"No," Otis said. "I mean... what if we were meant to?"

Trina looked at him through the rearview mirror. Just for a second.

Then she turned the music up.

But that look said more than she let on.

INT. SURVEILLANCE STATION – SAME TIME

Clarice leaned forward at the monitor. The party bus feed played, grainy but clear.

The Tall Man stood beside her.

"They're with the girl now."

"Trina," Clarice said, smiling faintly. "I always liked her."

"She doesn't know what they're carrying."

"No," Clarice said. "But she knows how to run. That's enough."

Otis settled into the seat of the party bus, the music drowning out his doubts. But in the quiet corners of his mind, he knew they were running headfirst into trouble. Each mile closer to Atlanta brought them deeper into a conspiracy they barely understood.

Chapter Six: On the Run

Otis, Leon, and Trina head north with no real plan, ducking highway cams and gas stations that feel like traps. They stash the case in a locked cabinet beneath a speaker box blasting music. Otis begins to suspect the device may not just be recognized by him — it may be responding to him.

They switch vehicles at a junkyard Trina "knows a guy" at. The guy doesn't ask questions but gives Otis a strange look after seeing the case. Leon starts noticing unmarked SUVs a little too often.

EXT. COUNTRY HIGHWAY – DAY

The landscape shifted from dense forest to open plains as the miles stretched on. The windows were cracked, the air still too thick, the engine too loud.

“How long do we keep driving before we run out of gas?” Leon asked, staring at the fuel gauge, which seemed to dip far too quickly.

Otis shrugged. “It’ll last as long as it takes for us to figure out who’s tracking us.”

“You think it’s her?” Leon asked, nodding toward Trina at the wheel.

Trina didn’t flinch. Her eyes were locked on the road.

“She’s a professional,” Otis said. “She’ll get us where we need to go.”

Leon didn't look convinced.

They passed the mile markers like numbers on a countdown, but they weren't sure if they were racing to something or away from it.

INT. JUNKYARD – LATER

Trina slammed the door of the van behind them. The guy she knew — a greasy mechanic with a tattoo of a rat on his neck — didn't ask for names. He just popped the hood of the car, glanced at the briefcase in the backseat, and gave them a look. A look that said, "I know what this is. I've seen it before."

"You sure you're not gonna leave it here?" Otis asked, but the mechanic just grinned, toothpick hanging from his lip.

"You got cash?"

"Yeah."

"Then I'll get you what you need."

As he fiddled with the engine, Leon stood by, watching the horizon. The junkyard seemed to stretch forever, and there was a strange quiet in the air, like someone was watching them — always watching.

EXT. DESERTED GAS STATION – AN HOUR LATER

The sun was setting in the rearview mirror, the orange sky bleeding into the horizon. They were running out of places to hide.

"How long before we get to Atlanta?" Leon asked, pulling a drink from the backseat cooler.

Otis didn't answer. Instead, he glanced at Trina, who kept driving as if she had a personal vendetta against the speed limit.

"You're avoiding the question," Leon said, suddenly wary.

"I'm just trying to stay ahead," Otis muttered. "Stay ahead of what's coming."

The case sat on the floor, between them, like it was breathing.

They all knew they couldn't outrun it.

INT. MOTEL ROOM – NIGHT

They checked into a cheap motel on the outskirts of a town that didn't even have a name. The clerk didn't even bother to look up when they handed over cash.

Otis tossed the briefcase onto the bed and stretched, running a hand over his face.

"We need to open it," he said, finally.

Trina had already cracked a beer and was sitting by the window, staring out into the parking lot.

"Not yet," she replied. "We don't know what it does."

"What if it's not just files?" Otis pressed.

Trina didn't respond, but Leon's eyes were glued to the case.

"We're already too deep," he said. "What's the worst that can happen?"

INT. OBSERVATION VAN – SAME TIME

The Tall Man watched from the shadows, his face illuminated only by the dim glow of the screen in front of him.

Clarice's voice crackled over the comms.

"What's their next move?"

"They'll head toward the backup location," the Tall Man answered. "And once they open the case, we'll have them."

Clarice smiled faintly.

"Good. We've been waiting too long."

Otis tightened his grip on the motel room's door handle, pulse racing. The world outside felt hostile, full of unseen eyes and unheard whispers. It was clear now—every step forward brought them closer to confrontation.

Chapter Seven: Intercepted

They get hit by a bounty crew — more organized this time. Not just muscle. Otis fights one and hears a phrase muttered into a comms unit: "Trask's asset is live." He doesn't know what it means.

They escape with injuries. Trina patches them up, curses a lot, and tells them they're going to need more than luck. She mentions a name: Ava — someone from Otis's dad's old world who "owes a few favors and maybe a kidney."

EXT. ABANDONED HIGHWAY – DAY

Otis wasn't the kind of guy to get caught off-guard. He was the one who usually controlled the chaos. But today?

Today was different.

"Otis noticed the fuel gauge nearing empty and felt a creeping anxiety. 'We need to find somewhere quiet to regroup,' he said sharply, glancing in the rearview mirror for any sign of pursuit. Leon nodded silently, indicating a roadside motel sign up ahead. They pulled the sedan off to the side, deciding it was safer to assess their next move rather than risk breaking down in an open stretch of road."

They were two miles past a dead town, nothing but dry brush and cracked asphalt around them. The beat-up sedan was parked off the side of the road, where an old motel stood like a forgotten ghost.

But someone had found them.

"Get out!" a voice shouted. Otis didn't look up.

Leon and Trina froze. The air felt still, too still. Then came the sound of boots — fast and purposeful.

Otis gripped the wheel tighter, just as a car screeched to a stop in front of them.

A woman in black stepped out, her face hidden behind mirrored sunglasses. A soldier's stance. Everything about her screamed "trained." She had that eerie calm, the kind that meant no one had told her she couldn't do something.

"We've got a situation," she said, voice even.

The man behind her stepped out, a larger figure wearing tactical gear. He cracked his knuckles, and the dark sunglasses made his expression unreadable.

"Ain't no one in the mood for this shit," Leon muttered under his breath.

"What do you want?" Otis demanded.

"You have something that belongs to us," the woman said, walking closer. "A device. And it's not just a case of losing it. We're talking consequences."

Otis gritted his teeth. He wasn't giving up the case. Not yet.

The tall man's voice came next: "Trask's asset is live."

Leon and Otis shared a look.

"What the hell is that supposed to mean?" Leon asked, his voice cutting through the silence.

The woman raised a hand, signaling to her crew. "It means, gentlemen, that you're now part of something much bigger than you understand."

INT. MOTEL ROOM – LATER THAT NIGHT

Trina's hands shook slightly as she dug through the first-aid kit. The adrenaline from the close call hadn't quite worn off yet. Her fingers were deft, though, sewing up the cuts without a second thought.

"The hell was that about?" she asked, though her voice was calmer than it should have been, considering.

Otis sat across from her, staring at the case as if it might come alive and bite him. "I don't know. But I think we're about to find out."

"Who are these people?" Leon asked. His voice was a little sharper than usual.

Trina just shrugged, still working on his arm. "Don't know, don't care. But they're not stopping. We need a plan."

"And what's the plan, then?" Leon shot back. "We keep running? Hope we find a safe spot? This isn't a road trip anymore, Trina. This is us running from a damn army."

Trina finished, set the needle down. "It's worse than an army, Leon."

Otis wasn't listening to them. His eyes were on the case, like it was whispering something to him.

INT. DARK ROOM – UNKNOWN LOCATION

Clarice sat in front of multiple monitors, her fingers flying over the keyboard. Her eyes flicked over the data, scanning, calculating.

She leaned back in her chair, a slow smile forming.

"It's time," she said softly. "Activate the next phase."

She glanced to her left, where the Tall Man stood silently, watching the feed. She didn't need to ask for confirmation. He was already in motion.

"The time's almost here. Prepare for the next step," she ordered. The words were cold, like everything about her.

Bruised but breathing, Otis leaned against the battered rental car. Ava's name echoed ominously in his mind, a ghost from his father's mysterious past. They had no choice left. They needed answers, even if those answers tore open wounds best left untouched.

Chapter Eight: Ava

Ava was cold. Sharp. Precise.

Her office — if you could even call it that — was more of a hideaway, a dimly lit space filled with old computers, tangled cables, and neon-green lights from hacking screens. The walls were cluttered with maps, photos, and cryptic data prints. It didn't look like much, but it had that underworld vibe that made you feel like you were on the edge of something important. Or something dangerous.

When Otis, Leon, and Trina stepped inside, Ava didn't greet them with warmth. She just nodded, gesturing for them to take a seat.

"So, you finally decided to bring the thing in."

Otis tossed the briefcase onto her cluttered desk, the click of the latch resonating in the small room.

"I don't trust anyone else to open it," he said.

Ava didn't say a word. She just reached for the briefcase, quickly unlocking it. Her hands were steady. Efficient. She didn't hesitate.

Inside the case was more than just files. A flash drive. A strange metal device. And a stack of manila folders.

Ava's eyes narrowed as she flipped through the contents. Her fingers hovered over the flash drive.

"You don't even know what this is, do you?" Ava asked, her voice like ice.

Otis didn't answer.

Ava took the flash drive and plugged it into a nearby computer. The screen flickered to life, showing an encrypted file. She studied it for a moment before pulling out a cable, attaching it to a second machine.

"Your father left this for you, didn't he?" Ava asked, as she typed furiously, bypassing layers of encryption with swift keystrokes.

Otis tensed.

"How do you know about my father?"

Ava's eyes met his for the first time. There was no emotion in her face, just facts.

"Everyone knows about him. He was the architect behind this — this program." She gestured to the screen. "Project Switch."

INT. ABANDONED LAB – LATER

The digital files started flooding in. Data streams. Blueprints. Classified programs. There was one name, one phrase that kept repeating: Project Switch. Ava clicked through layers of security, revealing one document after another. The truth started to surface.

"Your father was the brains behind a lot of this," Ava continued, her voice still flat. "This isn't just a set of files or a weapon. This is the framework for total control. You didn't just steal a briefcase, Otis. You're holding a digital time bomb."

Otis ran his hands over his bald head, the weight of the revelation crashing into him.

“What does it mean for me?” he asked.

Ava didn’t look up from the screen. She was in too deep now, following the data wherever it led her.

“You were always meant to be part of this,” she said, almost absentmindedly. “Your father set this all up, with you as the key. The key.”

Leon and Trina exchanged a glance.

“What happens now?” Trina asked, her tone wary.

Ava sat back in her chair and finally gave them her attention. Her gaze was icy, but there was something calculating in it. Something that suggested she knew more than she was willing to say.

“Now we get to work. You have no idea what you’ve started.”

EXT. ABANDONED LAB – LATER

The group left the lab with a new sense of urgency. They knew what they had, but not exactly what it would cost them.

Trina, always the practical one, spoke first.

“So what now? We just keep running, or are we actually doing something about this?”

Otis looked down at the briefcase, still unopened. He was the key. But to what?

"We find out what my father did," Otis said. "And we stop it before it stops us."

INT. DARK ROOM – UNKNOWN LOCATION

Clarice watched from the shadows, observing their every move. Her fingers twitched, her eyes locked on the footage of the lab.

"They've opened it," she said, her voice cold. The Tall Man stood beside her, not needing to ask who she meant.

"Now we wait," Clarice continued, her lips curling into a dangerous smile. "They've just become players in a game they don't understand."

The screen flashed again, showing Otis, Leon, and Trina's departure from the lab.

Clarice turned to the Tall Man, her eyes gleaming.

"Prepare them for the next phase," she ordered.

Watching the encrypted files flash across Ava's screens, Otis felt the shadows closing in. Secrets were never meant to stay hidden forever, and soon they'd have to confront the cost of uncovering them.

Chapter Nine: Static

They were ambushed again — this time during a file transfer. The attackers were ex-military. Ava fought back harder than expected. Trina disappears during the chaos.

Otis uses the device as bait and lures the attackers away. Leon saves his life. They lose half the data.

EXT. BACKROAD – DAY

Otis leaned against the side of their now-battered rental car, staring at the endless stretch of highway that seemed to mock them. The sun beat down, but his mind was elsewhere, lost in the storm of what they'd just survived.

Ava had cracked the code. She'd almost unlocked the final piece of the puzzle. They were so close, but then it happened.

They hadn't even seen it coming. The sound of footsteps — boots hitting gravel. Then, out of nowhere, a barrage of gunfire had shattered the quiet.

Leon had ducked first, pulling Otis to the ground. The military mercenaries who'd been tracking them had come out of the trees like wolves.

Otis had no time to think, only to react.

He grabbed the device, holding it up to the attackers. It was the only thing they wanted. And maybe — just maybe — it would buy him a few precious seconds.

INT. GAS STATION – EARLIER THAT DAY

Ava's hands flew over the keyboard. She was connected to the flash drive, eyes flicking between the code and the screens that were coming alive before her.

The atmosphere in the room had been quiet. Tense. Leon had been pacing, watching the door, while Trina was on the phone — probably making some deal or causing some chaos.

"It's almost done," Ava said, her voice tight. "I just need a few more minutes."

But then... the static.

The sound. The crackle that seemed to come out of nowhere, filling the room with a low hum. It was loud, louder than it should have been.

"Ava?" Leon asked, his voice rising. "What's going on?"

The screen flickered.

Ava looked at it, then back at Otis. "We're being watched," she muttered, her eyes darting to the corners of the room.

EXT. GAS STATION – CONTINUOUS

Otis heard it first — the unmistakable sound of engines.

"We've got company," Otis muttered. He looked at Leon. "Now, get in the car."

The others barely had time to react. They had no choice but to run.

But they didn't get far.

INT. BACKROOM – SAME TIME

Ava's screen flashed one last time, revealing the data.

And then, the screen went black.

"No!" Ava slammed her fist on the keyboard.

The door burst open. In came the ex-soldiers. They were dressed like they were fresh out of a military operation — tactical vests, blacked-out goggles. One of them carried a comms unit.

"Trask's asset is live," the mercenary said, his voice low and threatening.

"You've got to be kidding me," Leon swore.

EXT. WOODED AREA – DAY

Otis took the device and ran. He was too far ahead of Leon and Trina, but it was his only play.

"Otis!" Leon shouted, but Otis was already heading toward the trees, luring the attackers further away from the others.

The device in his hand felt like a ticking bomb.

It was always meant for him.

INT. DARK ROOM – UNKNOWN LOCATION

Clarice sat in front of a bank of monitors. The footage of Otis running with the device filled the screen.

Her fingers hovered over the controls, but she didn't press anything yet.

"He's too valuable," she whispered to herself, almost as if contemplating.

"He's ready," the Tall Man said from the shadows.

She nodded slowly. "Let's move."

EXT. WOODED AREA – LATER

Otis crouched behind a fallen log, the weight of the device heavy in his hands. He could hear the footsteps coming closer, and the mercenaries were right behind him. But there was one thing he was sure of — he wasn't going to make it out without getting what he wanted.

He pulled the device from his pocket and hit the button.

INT. GAS STATION – SAME TIME

Leon and Trina were already halfway back to the car, but they stopped short when the sound of a distant explosion shook the ground.

The flash of light could be seen through the trees, and a low rumble filled the air.

"What the hell did he do?" Leon muttered, his heart pounding in his chest.

EXT. WOODED AREA – LATER

Otis stumbled back to the gas station, dazed, covered in dirt.

He had lost the data — or half of it, at least. It didn't matter. They had the device. And they had a new enemy on their tail.

But the question lingered: Was it over? Or was this just the beginning?

Otis stared at the burning woods behind them, heart heavy. Trina was gone. The data was compromised. Yet amidst the loss, a new name—Raymond Trask—echoed as a beacon in the darkness. His father's legacy wasn't done with him yet.

Chapter Ten: Ghosts

Ava reveals what she knows about Otis's father — he didn't just go off the grid. He built the system Clarice hijacked. Otis is furious. Leon tries to ground him.

They follow a secondary trail: a rural trailer once used by Otis's dad. Inside, they find a second encrypted drive and a backup message. It points to a name: Raymond Trask.

EXT. SECLUDED ROAD – DAY

The old truck rattled as it bumped down the deserted road, gravel dust trailing in their wake. Otis had been quiet for a long time, eyes fixed out the window, his mind racing.

"You're sure we're going to find something there?" Leon asked, watching him closely.

Otis didn't answer. He wasn't sure himself. But there was something in his gut telling him that the rural trailer in the middle of nowhere was the key to everything. The key to his father's disappearance. The key to the digital weapon that had already changed their lives forever.

Ava sat in the front passenger seat, flipping through a folder of old documents.

"You're not going to find any easy answers," she said quietly. "What you're after is something that was buried for a reason."

“I'm not looking for easy answers. I'm looking for my father,” Otis snapped.

Leon gave him a sideways glance. "You sure? Because the more I dig into this, the more it feels like he's been gone for a reason."

Otis didn’t respond. His fists were clenched, knuckles white against the leather seat.

EXT. OLD TRAILER – LATER

The trailer sat at the edge of a forgotten field, barely visible among the overgrown grass and weeds. The paint was peeling, the windows cracked.

Otis stepped out first, the weight of the situation settling heavily on his shoulders. He felt the burn in his chest, the anger bubbling up again. This was where his father had once lived. Where he had spent the last few years of his life. And now, here it was, abandoned, forgotten, just like Otis had been.

He stepped onto the porch, his boots creaking under his weight. Trina stood beside him, keeping a wary eye on their surroundings. Leon was looking around, taking in the scene, trying to make sense of it all.

“I don’t know if this is the place,” Leon muttered. “Looks like someone just left.”

Ava came up behind them, scanning the area. She didn’t seem surprised. She wasn’t in a hurry to make any conclusions.

"This place was never meant to be found," she said. "Your father kept secrets. Big ones."

Otis felt a flash of guilt, but it was swallowed by rage. "Tell me something I don't know."

INT. OLD TRAILER – MOMENTS LATER

The inside of the trailer was darker than the outside, with only the dim light from the single window streaming in. Dust hung in the air, and the faint smell of mildew mixed with the old scent of forgotten memories.

Otis moved cautiously, his boots clicking on the wood floor. He looked around, hoping to find something — anything — that would give him answers.

Then he saw it.

A metal box hidden beneath the floorboards, almost deliberately concealed. It had scratches on the edges, like it had been shoved back into place too quickly.

His heart raced as he crouched down, peeling the floorboard back. He pulled the box out, almost reverently, and flipped the latch.

Inside was another encrypted drive — identical to the one they had taken from the casino. The same cold, dangerous weight.

A small note was tucked beneath it, handwritten, smudged but still legible.

"If you're reading this, the game has changed. You were always meant to carry this. The system is yours now. Stay hidden. Find Raymond Trask. He knows what comes next."

Otis stared at the name.

Raymond Trask.

His father's name was connected to all of this, and now there was someone else involved. Someone with answers.

EXT. OLD TRAILER – LATER

The group stood outside the trailer, the mystery of Otis's father's past pressing down on them. The wind had picked up, but it didn't offer any relief.

Ava spoke up, her voice calm but cold. "This isn't just about stopping Clarice. This is much bigger than you think."

Otis clenched the drive tightly. "I don't care how big it is. I want to find out what he did. I want to find out why I'm involved in this."

"You're involved because your father made you the key," Ava said, her eyes never leaving Otis. "And now you have to decide whether you'll unlock it or destroy it."

The weight of her words hit him harder than the sight of the drive in his hands.

INT. OBSERVATION VAN – SAME TIME

Clarice watched, coldly, as the footage of Otis and his team continued to play on the monitor. Her fingers traced the edge of the screen.

"They've found the trailer," the Tall Man said, his voice flat.

Clarice didn't respond immediately. She was too focused, watching Otis as he stood outside the trailer, holding the drive.

"Raymond Trask," the Tall Man added. "We've had him on our radar for years."

Clarice smiled faintly, her eyes glinting with a dangerous light.

"Then it's time we bring him in."

Holding the second encrypted drive, Otis felt a strange resolve. This wasn't merely about survival—it was about making a choice. A choice that would either honor his father's intentions or bury them forever.

Chapter Eleven: Ghost Protocol

Otis didn't know what to think anymore.

His father, a ghost. The case, a weapon of untold destruction. Raymond Trask, the name he'd never heard before, suddenly the next piece of a puzzle he was too deep into to stop. And with each step, it felt like the walls were closing in.

EXT. DOWNTOWN ATLANTA – DAY

Otis, Leon, and Trina were back in the city, blending in like just another group of lost travelers. But the weight of what they were carrying hung heavy. The encrypted drive. The secret his father left behind. And now, the looming presence of Raymond Trask.

They'd parked in a quiet alley and were walking through the crowded streets. People bustled past them, oblivious to the dangerous game being played just under the surface. They needed to find Trask.

But the closer they got to him, the more Otis felt like he was being drawn into something much bigger. The atmosphere was thick with tension, and the more he thought about it, the more he realized: this was never just about the briefcase.

It was about power. And control. And the legacy his father left behind.

"We should lay low," Leon muttered, glancing nervously around. "We don't even know what this guy's gonna want from us."

Trina was ahead of them, her phone in hand. "I'm getting a signal on him. He's close."

"We don't know what we're walking into," Leon warned again. But he was already moving, following Trina.

Otis just nodded, the tension rising in his chest. He couldn't ignore it anymore. He was in the center of something that had been spinning long before he showed up.

INT. RUNDOWN APARTMENT – LATER

The building looked abandoned, but there was a faint hum of life coming from inside. Old lights flickered. The smell of mildew mixed with the acrid scent of stale air.

Otis led the way, pushing open the door. Inside was a man sitting at a table. Raymond Trask.

He didn't look like what Otis expected. He wasn't a shadowy figure with a tie and a smooth voice. He was grizzled, unshaven, a man who looked like he'd spent too much time in the dark corners of the world.

"Otis Trask," Raymond said, looking up from the papers spread out before him. "Your father's son, huh?"

Otis stiffened. "You know my father?"

"Of course I do," Raymond replied, his voice rough but clear. "I knew him better than you ever will."

Trina stepped forward, eyes narrowed. "What is all this? What's really going on here?"

Raymond chuckled darkly. "It's not a game anymore. Your father built something. And now, you're the key to it all. The system, the files, the switch. The truth is, your father didn't just disappear. He went underground, built this whole operation so that it could survive. So that someone could take control when the time was right."

Otis looked at him, trying to digest the words. "And now that someone is me?"

Raymond nodded. "You don't get it yet. But you will."

INT. ABANDONED WAREHOUSE – SAME TIME

The Tall Man was watching everything unfold on a set of monitors, his face shadowed.

"They found Trask," he said, his voice low, almost to himself.

Clarice stepped out from the shadows, her eyes glinting with something dangerous. "Now it begins."

The Tall Man didn't need to ask for clarification. He knew what was coming.

EXT. WAREHOUSE DISTRICT – NIGHT

Otis stood with Raymond Trask, the encrypted drive in his hand. The wind howled through the broken windows, carrying with it the scent of rain. Trina and Leon were waiting in the shadows, eyes scanning the surroundings.

"It's all connected," Trask continued, his voice low. "Your father's work, the system, the weapon. Everything that's been happening is a result of his choices. And now, it's your turn to decide how it ends."

Otis felt the weight of those words pressing on him. This wasn't just a mission. It was his legacy. His father had built the system. And now it was up to Otis to decide whether to destroy it or control it.

"What happens if I don't follow through?" Otis asked, gripping the drive tighter.

Trask's lips twitched into a grim smile. "It's not about following through. It's about survival. You do what you have to do to stay alive. You turn the switch."

INT. DARK ROOM – SAME TIME

Clarice watched everything on the monitor, the lines of data flashing before her eyes. Her lips curled into a smile.

"It's time. Prepare for the next phase."

The Tall Man stood at her side, his expression unreadable.

Clarice's fingers danced over the keyboard, entering the final command. The pieces were in place.

"The game is in motion," she said quietly. "Let's see how they play."

Otis's jaw clenched tightly. Raymond Trask's revelations had rattled him, but clarity emerged in the chaos. They had a mission: dismantle the system or become another cog within it. There was no turning back now.

Chapter Twelve: The Black Site

The room was cold, sterile. The kind of place where the walls felt like they were closing in. Concrete floors, fluorescent lights flickering overhead, and nothing that spoke of life — just cold, hard systems, humming in the background like a living, breathing machine.

Otis, Leon, Trina, and Ava stood just inside the entrance, staring at the heavily fortified door ahead. Behind them, the hum of the facility was deafening. It wasn't a typical building. It wasn't even a typical site. It was a black site, a place hidden from everything and everyone.

No questions asked, no records kept.

Ava stepped forward, fingers tapping at the panel beside the door, scanning the biometric lock. The sound of keys clicking echoed in the silence.

"How long before they figure out we're here?" Leon asked, eyes darting nervously.

"Not long," Ava replied, her voice low but confident. "This place has a way of detecting intruders. But I've got the code."

She typed in a final sequence and the door clicked open with a soft, mechanical hum.

INT. BLACK SITE – MAIN CONTROL ROOM

Inside, the room was filled with monitors, servers, and terminals. Data flashed across the screens, systems working in sync to track every movement, every interaction. The heart of the operation was here.

"This is it," Ava muttered, her hands already flying over the keys. "The central command for Project Switch. This is where it all began."

Otis couldn't help but look around. There was something about the place that felt wrong — like they were trespassing in a world they shouldn't have entered. His father's work. The system he built. And now, here they were, in the belly of the beast.

"How do we stop it?" Otis asked.

Ava didn't answer immediately. She was focused on the screens, pulling up classified files that had been hidden behind layers of encryption.

"We don't stop it," she said after a long pause. "We destroy it. We burn it all down before it spreads."

"And how do we do that?" Leon asked, his voice edged with frustration.

Ava's fingers paused. She looked up at them, her expression grim.

"By hitting the core system. We disable the servers here, take out the backup servers offsite, and we fry everything. No recovery. No second chances."

Otis stood, his jaw tight. He was ready to move, to destroy it. But something was nagging at him.

Something about the system felt too controlled. Too well-guarded.

"Is there any chance they're already onto us?" Otis asked, turning to Ava.

Ava met his gaze, her face hardening. "Yes. But they don't know how close we are."

EXT. BLACK SITE – OUTSIDE

High above the black site, a drone hovered, its camera zooming in on the facility. Inside, the shadows of mercenaries moved, watching for any sign of intrusion.

Clarice's voice echoed through the secure line.

"Activate the security protocols," she commanded. "They're in the system."

The Tall Man nodded, his fingers quickly typing in commands.

"Already done," he said, watching the footage of Otis and the others inside the control room.

Clarice smiled to herself. They were getting closer, but they had no idea what they were really up against.

"Let them think they're in control," she whispered. "It'll be their last mistake."

INT. BLACK SITE – MAIN CONTROL ROOM

Ava continued typing, her eyes flicking over the data, watching the countdown.

"The core system is almost exposed," she said, "Just a few more—"

Suddenly, alarms blared. The room went from cold to chaotic in seconds. Red lights flashed as the walls around them seemed to pulse with the weight of the system locking them in.

"They know we're here," Ava said, panic creeping into her voice. "We have to move, now."

The door to the control room slammed shut with a deafening sound, locking them inside.

"We're trapped!" Leon shouted, moving toward the door, but the metal was solid. Nothing was getting through.

Otis turned to Ava. "How do we get out?"

Ava's eyes were frantic now. She grabbed the data drive they'd been after.

"We take this," she said, her voice shaking, "And we get the hell out of here. NOW!"

But just as she reached for the door to leave, it exploded open, throwing her and Leon back. The blast sent them flying across the room.

Otis was already on his feet, running to them, pulling them up. The room was a mess of alarms, flashing red, and the sound of boots slamming against the floor.

EXT. BLACK SITE – NIGHT

The helicopter whirred to life in the distance, kicking up dust as it landed, securing their escape.

"Move!" Otis shouted, pulling Leon and Ava to their feet, ready to leave before they were caught.

But they weren't alone.

The Tall Man stepped from the shadows, flanked by two armed mercenaries.

"You're not going anywhere," he said, his voice ice cold.

The explosion's echo faded, leaving them breathless but unbroken. Otis knew they had crossed a point of no return. This wasn't just about escaping anymore—it was about fighting back.

Chapter Thirteen: Ghosts of War

The blast had thrown them off course, but they weren't done yet. Otis, Leon, and Ava staggered to their feet, their heads pounding from the blast. They had to move fast, but every second felt like they were running out of time.

The helicopter was their only chance, but the Tall Man and his mercenaries were closing in.

EXT. BLACK SITE – NIGHT

The air was thick with smoke, and the sound of heavy boots grew louder behind them. Otis's heart pounded in his chest as he pulled Ava and Leon toward the waiting helicopter. The roar of the rotors filled the air, drowning out everything else.

"Get in!" Otis yelled over the noise, pushing them toward the open door.

They didn't hesitate. Leon climbed in first, followed by Ava, but Otis stopped, turning around to face the Tall Man.

The Tall Man's eyes narrowed, and his lips curled into a cold smile.

"You think you can outrun this?" he asked, his voice low and dangerous.

Otis didn't answer. He knew what was at stake, and he wasn't about to let it end here. He ducked into the helicopter and slammed the door shut behind him.

The helicopter shot into the air, gaining altitude as the Black Site grew smaller in the distance. The ground below looked distant, far away — like a life that was already slipping through his fingers.

INT. HELICOPTER - MOVING

As they flew toward safety, the weight of what had just happened began to settle in. Otis stared out of the window, his mind racing. They had just barely escaped the Black Site, but they weren't free yet.

Ava was still reeling from the explosion, her hands trembling as she clutched the data drive.

"This… this is what your father left behind?" she asked, looking at Otis.

Otis nodded. "It's everything. The weapon. The system. The key to everything."

"I've never seen anything like it," Ava said quietly. "This could change the world."

Leon was silent for a moment, then spoke up.

"But we still don't know exactly what it does," he said, his voice low and tense. "What's the point of all this if we can't control it?"

Otis met his gaze. "We control it by stopping it."

EXT. OVERHEAD - NIGHT

The helicopter flew over dark, empty land, the lights of distant cities barely visible. They were heading for an unknown location, a place where they could regroup and figure out their next move. But Otis knew it wouldn't be long before they were being hunted again.

Clarice wouldn't stop. Not until she had what she wanted.

And the Tall Man? He was the ghost in the machine — the one pulling the strings from behind the scenes. If they wanted to end this, they'd have to deal with him first.

INT. SAFEHOUSE – LATER THAT NIGHT

They arrived at a small, secure location on the outskirts of the city. A nondescript house, a safe place where they could lay low for a while.

Inside, the tension didn't ease. If anything, it grew heavier as they gathered around the table, the encrypted drive at the center.

"We need to decrypt it," Ava said, setting up her laptop. "There's no more running."

Otis nodded, but the uncertainty in his chest didn't leave. He had the key now, but what would it unlock? And what would it cost them to stop it?

They couldn't afford to fail. Not now. Not with everything on the line.

INT. DARK ROOM – UNKNOWN LOCATION

Far away, deep in the shadows, Clarice stood in front of a series of monitors, her eyes locked on the footage of Otis and his team.

She knew they were getting closer, but it didn't matter. This wasn't about the device anymore. This was about control. The power to decide the fate of everything.

Her fingers hovered over the keyboard as the screen blinked in front of her. The Tall Man entered the room, his expression unreadable.

"They're still moving," the Tall Man said. "We lost them at the Black Site."

Clarice didn't look up. She was already typing in commands, her mind sharp, focused.

"We won't lose them again," she said. Her voice was cold, calculating. "We've just begun the real game."

EXT. SAFEHOUSE – NIGHT

Outside, the wind howled, but Otis felt nothing. He was numb, lost in the storm of everything that was happening. There was no turning back now.

They were at the heart of it all, standing at the threshold of something bigger than any of them realized.

The only question was: Would they survive it?

As the helicopter rose, Otis felt the world tilt beneath them. They had struck a blow, but the war was just beginning. Clarice and the Tall Man still loomed; dangers not easily evaded.

Chapter Fourteen: The Black Site

The safehouse had been quiet for hours. Too quiet.

Otis paced the room, his mind running a thousand miles a minute. The encrypted drive sat on the table in front of him, taunting him with its secrets. The questions kept multiplying: What was his father involved in? What did Project Switch mean? And most importantly, why was he the key?

Ava sat across from him, typing away at her laptop, her face illuminated by the glow of the screen. Leon leaned against the wall, arms crossed, watching the two of them. Trina had gone outside for a cigarette, giving them all a moment of peace, but it wouldn't last.

The silence between them was thick with the weight of their situation.

"Any luck?" Otis asked, breaking the silence.

Ava glanced up at him, her eyes tired but determined.

"I'm getting close," she replied. "But this isn't just encrypted data. It's something more. Your father didn't just leave files behind — he left a blueprint. A map."

Leon walked over, peering at the screen over Ava's shoulder.

"A map for what?"

"For control," Ava said softly. "For taking over the system. Every line of code, every system in place, it's all connected. Your father built something bigger than just a weapon — he built a network. A network of power. And it's alive."

Otis felt the weight of her words, like a hundred pounds of steel dropping onto his chest. His father wasn't just a man who disappeared. He wasn't just a man who made a weapon. He had built a system. And it wasn't just meant to survive; it was meant to evolve.

"So what now?" Leon asked, frustration creeping into his voice. "How do we stop this?"

Ava didn't answer immediately. She typed furiously, the clicking of the keys echoing in the silence. After a moment, she leaned back in her chair.

"We don't stop it," she said, her voice low. "We destroy it."

Otis clenched his jaw. "And how do we do that?"

"We take out the heart of the system," Ava said, eyes locked on the screen. "The core server. Once we do that, we erase everything. All the data, all the backups — gone. No recovery."

Otis nodded, but doubt lingered in his mind. It wasn't that simple. Nothing ever was. But they didn't have much of a choice. The more they learned, the more they realized how deep this went.

"Where do we find this 'core server'?" Leon asked.

Ava clicked through more files, pulling up a map of what appeared to be a facility.

"It's at a black site. An off-the-grid location. A place so secure that even if you had the coordinates, you wouldn't be able to get in without clearance."

Otis felt the gravity of it. This was bigger than they thought. Bigger than just stopping Clarice. This was about shutting down the whole operation — a mission that would either kill them or change everything.

"We'll need to move fast," Ava added, "But we won't be able to get inside easily. This site is equipped with military-grade security. It's as black as it gets."

Leon grunted. "So, we're sneaking in, guns blazing, and hoping we don't die?"

Ava didn't flinch. "Pretty much."

EXT. SAFEHOUSE – NIGHT

The group left the safehouse in the dead of night, under the cover of darkness. The streets were empty, and the only sounds were their footsteps and the low hum of their engine.

Otis couldn't help but feel like they were racing against time. Racing against an enemy they didn't fully understand. But they couldn't afford to hesitate now.

They were about to face the very heart of the system his father built. And if they didn't succeed, nothing would stop it.

"We need to be ready for anything," Otis said, his voice steady. "No more second chances."

INT. BLACK SITE – LATER

The facility stood before them, towering and imposing in the darkness. They'd reached the coordinates Ava had pulled from the data, but getting inside would be the real challenge.

It was a ghost facility, hidden from the world, accessible only to those with the highest-level clearance. The kind of place that didn't exist in any public records. The kind of place where people went in — but didn't come out.

"This is it," Ava said, her voice low as she surveyed the perimeter. "We're in. But we need to move fast."

They all knew what was at stake. No more running. No more hiding. They had to go in and finish what they started.

They approached the entrance, their steps quick and quiet. Leon held his breath, keeping his eyes peeled for any sign of movement.

The door was locked, but Ava was already working on it, her fingers dancing across the lockpad. After a tense moment, the door clicked open.

"Let's go," Ava whispered, her voice sharp.

Otis led the way, his heart pounding as they moved deeper into the facility.

INT. CORE SERVER ROOM – MOMENTS LATER

The core server room was as cold and sterile as the rest of the facility. A single row of servers hummed with life, blinking lights flashing in synchronized rhythms. This was it — the heart of the operation.

But just as Otis stepped forward, ready to destroy everything, the sound of footsteps echoed behind him.

"They're here," Ava said, her voice tight. "We don't have much time."

Otis glanced around quickly. The servers were already starting to power down, but it wasn't enough. The Tall Man and his mercenaries were closing in.

They had to finish what they started.

"Do it!" Otis shouted to Ava.

INT. HALLWAY – SAME TIME

The Tall Man stood at the end of the hallway, his gun drawn and aimed straight at Otis. He'd seen it before. He knew the play.

"It's over, Trask," the Tall Man said, his voice low and cold. "You're not getting out of here."

Otis watched the countdown tick to zero, feeling every second like a pulse. They had unleashed a storm—but he knew the real battle had only just begun.

Chapter Fifteen: Fallout

The gunshot rang out, deafening in the silence of the server room. Otis had no time to react. The Tall Man's voice echoed down the hallway.

"Give it up, Otis. You can't win this."

The sound of boots approached, too fast, too certain. Otis's mind raced, but he knew there was only one thing they could do — they had to finish this.

Ava's fingers were moving at lightning speed on the control panel, her face illuminated by the glow of the monitor. Leon was at the door, peering out, every nerve on edge. Trina was still at the rear, covering their backs.

"Ava!" Otis shouted. "Hurry up!"

Ava didn't respond, but Otis could see the beads of sweat on her forehead. This wasn't just hacking — this was a battle against time. If they didn't destroy the core system now, everything they'd worked for would fall apart.

The lights flickered as Ava bypassed the last layer of security.

"Got it!" Ava yelled, slamming her hand onto the button. The screens flashed, and then the countdown began.

A red light blinked on.

Thirty seconds.

"We need to move!" Leon shouted. "Now!"

But just as they turned to run, the Tall Man and his men appeared in the doorway. The mercenaries moved in quickly, weapons raised.

Otis reached for the gun at his waist. He'd been in tight situations before, but this was different. They were cornered, and the countdown had already begun.

EXT. BLACK SITE – NIGHT

Outside, the storm was picking up. The wind howled through the trees, the air thick with tension. The helicopter that had dropped them off earlier was still waiting, but the path to it was blocked by a wall of armed soldiers, their weapons aimed at Otis and his team.

Clarice stood in the distance, watching through a set of binoculars. Her face was hidden in the shadows, but her smile was unmistakable.

"Let them play their game," she murmured to the Tall Man, who had stepped up beside her. "We've got this."

The Tall Man nodded, his eyes narrowing as he focused on the group inside the facility.

"Once the data's gone, they'll have nothing left. They won't be able to run."

Clarice's lips twisted into a grin. "Exactly. And that's when we'll finish what we started."

INT. SERVER ROOM – CONTINUOUS

Otis's heart was racing. The countdown was ticking down, but they weren't out of the room yet. The mercenaries were closing in.

"Ava, tell me you've disabled the backups!" Otis shouted.

Ava didn't answer. She was too busy, too focused, trying to shut everything down. She didn't even look up, her fingers moving over the keyboard with mechanical precision.

"Almost there," she said, breathless.

The seconds felt like hours. Otis could see Leon tense, ready for a fight. Trina had already pulled a second weapon from her jacket, her eyes scanning the room for threats.

The Tall Man's voice was clear, cutting through the air like a knife.

"You're out of time, Trask."

Otis didn't flinch. He couldn't afford to. If they didn't destroy the system now, it was over.

The screen blinked once more — "DESTRUCTION INITIATED."

Ava slammed her hand onto the keyboard, her face set with determination. "It's done."

The explosion was immediate.

EXT. BLACK SITE – SAME TIME

Outside, the building trembled. The sound of explosions shook the ground, and the night sky was briefly lit up by the bright flare of the blast.

"It's done," Clarice said, her smile fading slightly. "They're finished."

But even as the flames rose into the air, there was no sense of relief. Not yet.

INT. SERVER ROOM – CONTINUOUS

The explosion rattled the room, but Otis didn't move. He knew it was over. He'd heard the system crumble. They'd wiped it all out.

But the room wasn't empty.

"Run!" Leon shouted, pulling Otis to his feet.

As they rushed for the exit, the room filled with a bright, blinding light.

And in the chaos, everything seemed to freeze. The Tall Man's voice rang out once again.

"This is far from over, Trask. You can't escape what's coming."

Otis didn't stop. They couldn't stop. Not now.

EXT. BLACK SITE - NIGHT

They emerged into the open air, the night air thick with smoke and the smell of fire. The helicopter was waiting, but it wasn't just waiting for them. It was a trap.

They were surrounded. Soldiers in tactical gear were everywhere, weapons aimed, moving in on them.

Otis's pulse raced as the soldiers tightened their circle. There was no way out.

"You don't need to do this," Otis said, stepping forward. His voice was calm, but he knew this was their last stand.

The soldier closest to him raised his rifle, but before he could pull the trigger, Trina acted.

In an instant, the air was filled with the sound of gunfire. It was chaos. The soldiers scattered, returning fire. Leon grabbed Otis, pulling him toward the helicopter.

"Go! Go now!" Leon shouted.

Otis stumbled forward, adrenaline pumping through his veins. The helicopter blades roared, and as the door closed behind them, they took off into the sky —

leaving the Black Site, and whatever was left behind, to burn.

INT. HELICOPTER – NIGHT

They were in the air, and the ground below was disappearing fast. Otis glanced out the window, his mind still reeling.

"What now?" Trina asked, her eyes cold, scanning the sky.

"Now we get answers," Otis said, his voice low. "But we don't stop running."

Leon nodded. "The war's just begun."

Otis stared at the chaos left behind, the helicopter soaring through the night. They had barely escaped, and yet he felt certain they'd just stirred the hornet's nest. Now, every loose end mattered, every moment crucial. The fires below may have died, but in his chest, the burn still lived. Clarice wasn't finished. The system wasn't dead. And Otis knew one thing for sure: before this ended, they'd have to tie off every thread—and bury the ones still moving.

Chapter Sixteen: Loose Ends

The helicopter sped through the night, cutting through the air like a shadow on a mission. But Otis couldn't shake the feeling that they were still trapped — even in the sky. The system they had destroyed wasn't just a collection of files and data; it was a beast, and they had only scratched the surface.

Ava sat at the back of the helicopter, her eyes glued to the screen of a portable computer. The rest of the team was silent, lost in their own thoughts. Leon stared out the window, watching the blur of the landscape pass beneath them, while Trina kept a watchful eye on the perimeter, her hand never far from her gun.

"What now?" Leon asked, his voice low.

Otis didn't answer at first. He was thinking, trying to piece everything together. They had destroyed the system, but something told him it wasn't over. Clarice had too much power. The Tall Man was still out there. The loose ends had yet to be tied up.

"We need to find out what's left," Otis finally said. "There's something we're missing."

Ava looked up from her screen, her face pale from the glow of the monitor.

"I've been going through what we got," she said. "And I don't think it's over. I think we've just triggered the next phase of Project Switch."

Otis's eyes narrowed. "What does that mean?"

"It means," Ava began, "that we've been part of something bigger than we realized. Your father's work wasn't just about surveillance or control. It was about a network. A program. And it's been evolving for years."

INT. HELICOPTER – NIGHT – MOMENTS AFTER ESCAPE

Otis's phone buzzed. Unknown number. He hesitated, then answered.

"Otis Trask speaking."

A clipped voice came through the line.
"Mr. Trask, this is Franklin Murray, Systems Supervisor, Wright-Patterson. I've been attempting to reach you through official channels."

Otis blinked. "Frank? Didn't recognize the number."

"You've missed two classified briefings and a secure login checkpoint. Your clearance status has triggered a level-two review. I'm calling to confirm your operational status and location."

Otis glanced at Leon, who was already mouthing, *"NSA?"*

"Frank, I'm in the middle of a personal situation. Can't say much."

A pause.

"I assumed as much. I will put you in for a week of annual leave. Keep us informed if your situation changes."

Otis exhaled. "Yes sir." Then ended the call.

Leon raised an eyebrow. "That sounded... serious."

Trina smirked. "And here I thought you were just freelancers."

EXT. ABANDONED MILITARY BASE – NIGHT

The helicopter touched down on a small, desolate airstrip. The base ahead was abandoned, its rusted gates long since closed, but the hangars in the distance still stood, like ghosts of a past they couldn't erase.

"This is it," Trina said as she peered out the side window. "The loose end you're looking for."

The group disembarked, heading toward the dilapidated base. The air was thick with tension, but they had no choice. They needed to find out where the backup servers were hidden — and more importantly, what remained of Project Switch.

INT. MILITARY BASE – NIGHT

The door to the base creaked open, revealing a dark interior. It was the kind of place that felt abandoned but still alive in some twisted way — the hum of old equipment, the buzz of long-forgotten systems.

"What are we looking for?" Leon asked, his voice cutting through the eerie quiet.

Ava led the way, pulling out a map from the data they'd gathered earlier.

"We need to get to the old mainframe. The core backup servers are still in operation here, despite everything. They were hidden deep underground."

Otis's chest tightened. The thought of facing whatever remained of the system that had haunted them felt like diving into the heart of darkness. But he had no choice.

"Let's get to it," Otis said, his voice low.

EXT. BASE - NIGHT

The group made their way through the maze of darkened buildings, every creak of the floorboards amplifying the tension. The deeper they went, the more they realized how deep the system ran. It wasn't just a weapon. It was a global network, built to span continents, infiltrating everything from governments to corporations.

Ava was ahead of them, her fingers moving quickly over a series of control panels. She was close.

"Almost there," she said, glancing over her shoulder. "But I don't know how much longer we have before they realize we're here."

Just as she spoke, the sound of footsteps echoed from the hallway.

"We've got company," Trina said, her voice sharp. She ducked behind a nearby wall, motioning for the rest to follow.

Leon took cover next to Otis, his hand on his gun.

The footsteps were getting closer, and Otis knew they didn't have long. He didn't know who was coming, but it didn't matter. They had to finish this.

INT. UNDERGROUND FACILITY – NIGHT

Ava finally reached the mainframe. The room was vast and cold, filled with old servers that hummed to life as soon as they entered. Screens blinked on, showing data they could barely begin to understand.

"Here," Ava said, breathing hard. "This is the heart of it. If we destroy this, everything goes with it."

Otis stood in front of her, taking it all in. This was the endgame.

"How do we destroy it?" Leon asked, his eyes scanning the room for any signs of danger.

Ava moved quickly, tapping in commands on the terminal.

"This is the last step. Once we cut the connection, everything collapses."

"What's left?" Otis asked, his voice tight. He needed to know everything now.

Ava hesitated before answering.

"Once this system is gone, we don't just lose Project Switch. We lose everything connected to it. Every black site, every surveillance system, every ... everything."

Leon's eyes widened. "So it's not just about stopping Clarice."

"No," Ava said, her voice darkening. "It's about stopping everything."

EXT. MILITARY BASE – NIGHT

Outside, the sky was dark, but the storm was coming — fast. The winds picked up, and the temperature dropped. It felt like the world itself was shifting, like they were standing on the precipice of something far bigger than they had ever imagined.

Otis glanced back at Ava, who was still working on the terminal. They didn't have much time left.

"Do it," Otis said.

Ava hit the final key.

The lights flickered.

The ground beneath them trembled.

Then everything went dark.

Otis stepped onto the cracked tarmac, eyes scanning the hollow base ahead. The night might have bought them time, but not peace. Answers waited beneath that rusted roof, and somewhere in that silence, the past was preparing to speak.

Chapter Seventeen: Playback

The silence in the underground facility was deafening after the explosion of lights. The server room had gone dark, leaving only the flickering emergency lights above them. It felt like the world was holding its breath. But Otis couldn't shake the feeling that something was wrong — that they hadn't really finished what they'd started.

Ava was staring at the terminal, her fingers frozen above the keyboard.

"What the hell happened?" Leon asked, his voice shaky with anxiety. He glanced around the dark room, scanning for any signs of movement.

Ava didn't respond immediately. She was too focused on the screen in front of her. When she finally spoke, her voice was low, almost hesitant.

"We didn't just destroy the system. We... activated something else."

Otis's heart skipped a beat. "What do you mean, activated?"

"Look," Ava said, turning the screen toward them. The data was still scrambled, but it was different from the files they'd seen before. This wasn't just code. This was something else — something alive.

The lines of text were shifting, changing. Almost as if they were responding to the input. Ava typed quickly, trying to trace the anomaly.

"It's like a feedback loop," Ava muttered, her voice tense. "We destroyed the core, but the system was designed to adapt. It's... adapting."

The room grew colder. Otis could feel the weight of it pressing in on him. They had thought they were close to the end, but now everything felt like it was spiraling out of control.

"What's happening?" Leon asked again, more forcefully this time.

Ava swallowed hard, her fingers pausing over the keyboard.

"It's replaying," she said softly. "A backup. A... contingency protocol. Your father had a failsafe. And I think... it's trying to rebuild itself."

Otis's stomach turned. "We didn't stop it."

"No," Ava said, shaking her head. "We triggered it. It's playing back everything we deleted."

INT. CONTROL ROOM – SAME TIME

Outside the facility, deep within the heart of the operation, Clarice stood in front of a series of monitors, watching the playback unfold. The data was flooding in, confirming what she had feared.

"It's begun," she said, her voice a low whisper. She leaned closer to the screen, her eyes gleaming with cold satisfaction.

The Tall Man stood behind her, watching silently. His expression was unreadable, but the tension in the air was palpable.

"This was always the plan," Clarice continued, her lips curling into a dangerous smile. "Trask's legacy wasn't just a weapon. It was a system. And now, the system has evolved."

"What do you need from me?" the Tall Man asked, his voice gruff.

"Nothing yet," Clarice replied. "For now, we wait."

The screens before them flickered with life, and Clarice's fingers hovered over the controls.

"Let them think they've won. They won't understand until it's too late."

EXT. MILITARY BASE – NIGHT

The storm outside had picked up, the wind howling through the abandoned buildings of the base. But inside, the team was trapped in a different kind of storm. They had destroyed the system, but it wasn't done with them. Not yet.

Leon paced back and forth, his nerves frayed.

"We're running out of time," he muttered.

Trina glanced over at him, her arms crossed. "If we don't fix this, we're all dead."

Otis stood near Ava, watching the screen as she typed furiously. The data was still shifting, still changing. The feedback loop was like a living thing — constantly adapting, always one step ahead.

"How do we stop this?" Otis asked, his voice tight.

Ava didn't look up. She was too absorbed in the terminal, her fingers moving faster now, almost desperately.

"I don't know," she admitted, her voice breaking slightly. "It's like the system is... alive. It keeps regenerating itself."

Otis's chest tightened. They couldn't fight an enemy that was constantly changing.

"We need to cut it off at the source," he said, his voice sharp. "There's a secondary backup somewhere. A place my father set up. We have to get there before it's too late."

INT. DARK ROOM – UNKNOWN LOCATION

Clarice sat in front of her monitors, the flickering lights casting strange shadows across her face. She had what she wanted. The system was responding to the input, coming to life again.

But there was something else beneath the surface. A whisper. A new voice — one she hadn't anticipated.

"It's growing," she murmured, her eyes narrowing. "Faster than I thought."

The Tall Man stepped forward, his face unreadable.

"We can't allow it to get ahead of us," he said. "We can't let it evolve too much."

Clarice looked up at him, her lips curling into a faint smile.

"It's already done. There's no turning back now."

EXT. MILITARY BASE – NIGHT

Outside, the wind howled louder, the storm reaching a fever pitch. Otis, Leon, Trina, and Ava stood by the entrance to the base, their minds racing with the knowledge that they were facing something they didn't fully understand.

"Let's move," Otis said, his voice filled with determination. "We can't let it reach full capacity."

Ava nodded, still looking at the terminal as if trying to make sense of what was happening. The feedback loop was intensifying, the data more chaotic now. The system was alive — and they were running out of time to stop it.

"We need to find the source and shut it down, now," Ava said. "Before it learns how to adapt again."

Otis turned to lead the group toward the next phase. He knew the stakes were higher now, and with every passing minute, the world they knew was slipping further out of their control. They weren't just up against Clarice anymore. They were up against the legacy of a system his father had built — a system that was far more dangerous than anyone had realized.

The base was behind them, but the burden wasn't. Every step they took away from it was weighted with truths that couldn't be unlearned. Otis gripped the drive tighter—this wasn't just a story about control. It was about inheritance.

Chapter Eighteen: The Detour

They were on the move again, but this time it wasn't just a race to escape. This time, they were headed straight into the heart of the operation — the final backup facility. The place where the last remnants of Otis's father's work were hidden. The place where the system could be destroyed once and for all.

But as they drove toward the coordinates, Otis couldn't shake the feeling that they were being led into a trap. It was too clean, too easy. And that nagging voice in the back of his head wasn't letting him rest.

"We're close," Ava said, glancing at the map on her phone. "The backup facility is just ahead."

Trina was driving, her eyes focused on the road. The hum of the engine and the quiet night outside felt surreal, as if the world had paused for a moment before they reached their destination.

Leon sat in the back, his hands clenched into fists. He was clearly anxious, but who could blame him? The stakes were higher now. They weren't just fighting for their survival anymore. They were fighting to stop Clarice and the system from taking over everything.

"I still don't like this," Leon muttered, looking out the window. "It feels too damn easy."

Otis didn't respond at first. He was lost in his thoughts, trying to anticipate what came next. They'd already gone through so much — why hadn't it ended yet?

"It's not easy," Otis finally said, his voice tight. "It's a setup."

Trina didn't look over, but her tone was flat. "I thought you were done with second-guessing."

Otis turned toward the window, watching the road ahead. His mind was running through all the possibilities. Could they really take down Project Switch? Could they stop Clarice?

A voice interrupted his thoughts, distant and cold.

"You're almost there," Ava said, breaking the silence. "Get ready."

EXT. BACKUP FACILITY – NIGHT

The backup facility was nestled deep in the woods, hidden by trees and a network of old security measures. It was the last place anyone would think to look.

As they parked the car near the entrance, the facility loomed in front of them — a concrete building, surrounded by high fences, with only a few lights flickering in the distance.

"Stay sharp," Otis warned, his eyes scanning the perimeter. They were walking straight into enemy territory, and he had no illusions about how this was going to go down.

Ava led the way, her hands steady as she worked to disable the security system at the gate. Leon and

Trina flanked Otis, keeping an eye out for anything out of the ordinary.

"This is it," Ava said, glancing back at the group. "Once we get inside, there's no turning back."

They all nodded, knowing what was at stake. There was no more running, no more hiding. They had to finish it.

The door opened with a soft click, and they slipped inside.

INT. BACKUP FACILITY – MAIN HALL

Inside, the facility was eerily quiet. The walls were lined with rows of computers, and the air smelled faintly of dust and oil. It was clear that this place had been abandoned for a while, but the equipment was still running.

"We're too late," Leon muttered, looking at the row of monitors, each one blinking with activity. "They're here."

Ava was already moving, her fingers flying over the controls as she tried to access the mainframe.

"They're watching us," Ava said, her voice tight. "The system has adapted. It's alive."

"We can't stop it?" Trina asked, moving toward a control panel nearby.

"Not with a simple shutdown," Ava replied. "We'll need to take out the core servers. But Clarice will be here any minute."

Otis looked at the door behind them, his pulse quickening. They had come so far. There was no turning back now.

Suddenly, the lights went out.

"Damn it," Leon swore, reaching for his flashlight.

A low hum vibrated through the room, the sound of the system beginning to wake. The walls seemed to pulse, the hum becoming louder, like the very building itself was alive.

"It's starting," Ava said, backing away from the terminal. "We have to move, now."

They rushed through the hallways, trying to find the main control room. But just as they turned a corner, they found themselves face to face with Clarice's mercenaries.

"You really thought you could escape this?" one of the men sneered, raising his gun.

But before Otis could react, Trina fired.

The mercenaries dropped to the floor, silent, motionless.

"We keep moving," Trina said, her voice low. "Clarice will be here soon."

INT. MAIN CONTROL ROOM – NIGHT

They finally reached the heart of the facility — the main control room. The walls were lined with rows of screens, and in the center stood a massive console, blinking with unreadable data.

"This is it," Ava said, breathing hard as she approached the console. "We disable this, and we shut everything down."

But as she moved toward it, the lights flickered again.

The backup facility hummed louder, almost as if it were warning them.

"Hurry," Otis said, stepping toward the door. "Clarice is here."

EXT. BACKUP FACILITY – SAME TIME

Clarice watched from the shadows, her eyes glowing with a dark satisfaction. She knew what was coming, and she wasn't worried. She had played the game long enough to know when it was her turn to strike.

"It's over," she whispered to herself. "This time, they won't escape."

The rain had started to fall, soft at first, then like needles. The streets ahead blurred in the downpour, but Otis's purpose was crystal clear. There would be no more hiding from ghosts. It was time to confront them.

Chapter Nineteen: The Betrayal

The air was thick with the hum of machines, and the blinking lights seemed to mock them. Ava stood at the console, fingers flying over the keys as she tried to work faster than the growing sense of dread gnawing at her. Otis watched her, his pulse quickening with every passing second. The backup facility was crumbling, and they had no idea what was coming next.

"Hurry up!" Leon shouted, his voice tense as he kept watch by the door.

Ava glanced at him, her face pale, sweat beading on her forehead. "I'm doing the best I can, but this system is more complicated than I thought. It's got layers of encryption, fail-safes… everything."

"We don't have time for everything!" Otis said, his voice low and urgent.

The sound of footsteps echoed through the hallway. Otis's instincts kicked in, his hand instinctively reaching for the gun at his waist.

"We're out of time," he muttered. "They're coming."

Ava looked up from the screen, her face tight. "We're close. Just give me another minute."

"No," Trina said, stepping forward. "We don't have a minute."

Before anyone could react, the door to the control room flew open, and a team of mercenaries flooded the room. Guns raised. Eyes cold.

Clarice stood in the doorway, her eyes locking onto Otis with cold, calculating precision.

"I warned you," she said, her voice steady and calm. "This is bigger than you. Bigger than all of you."

Otis gritted his teeth, eyes narrowing. "This ends now."

"It does," Clarice said, her lips curling into a small smile. "But not the way you think."

INT. CONTROL ROOM – SAME TIME

The tension in the room was unbearable. Otis stood in front of Ava, Leon at his side, while Trina had already moved to the back, her eyes scanning for any possible escape route. But there was no escaping this.

Clarice's mercenaries moved in, their weapons trained on the team. Ava's fingers hovered over the console, but she was frozen in place. The weight of the situation was too much. They had come so far, but now they were trapped.

"You think you can just walk away from this?" Clarice asked, stepping forward. "You think you can destroy something you don't understand?"

Otis's fists clenched at his sides. "We understand enough."

"You understand nothing," Clarice replied, her smile widening. "You never did."

Ava's eyes widened as she looked at the screen. The data was changing again. Shifting. Rebuilding itself.

"It's… it's adapting," she said, her voice shaking. "It's not gone. It's still alive."

Clarice's smile grew darker. "That's right. Your father's legacy isn't something you can destroy. It was designed to evolve. To survive."

Otis felt the anger boiling in him. She'd won. But not completely. He wasn't going to let her have everything.

"You're not taking it," Otis spat. "Not this time."

Clarice raised an eyebrow, clearly amused. "Oh? And how do you plan to stop me, Otis?"

Without warning, Trina stepped forward, her gun raised. She fired twice, the sound of the shots deafening in the small room. The mercenaries fell to the floor, their bodies crumpling with a sickening thud.

"Run," Trina shouted. "Now!"

Otis grabbed Ava's arm, pulling her toward the door. Leon followed quickly, Trina covering their backs as they rushed down the hallway.

EXT. BACKUP FACILITY – NIGHT

They burst out of the control room and into the darkened halls of the facility. The lights were flickering now, casting long shadows along the walls. Their footsteps echoed in the silence, quick and urgent.

"This way!" Ava shouted, leading the group down a narrow corridor. "We need to reach the server room — the core backup."

"How much farther?" Leon asked, his voice tight with frustration.

"Not far," Ava said. "We're almost there."

But as they turned a corner, they came face to face with more mercenaries. The hallway was blocked.

Otis didn't hesitate. He drew his gun and fired. The first mercenary went down, but there were too many. They were surrounded.

"Get to the server room!" Ava screamed. "I'll hold them off."

Otis hesitated, but Trina grabbed his arm and yanked him forward.

"We don't have time!" she shouted.

INT. SERVER ROOM – SAME TIME

They reached the server room, but Ava was already behind them, struggling to keep the door closed. She was running out of time, and they were running out of options.

"Ava!" Otis shouted. "We can't let them get us!"

But just as they thought they were safe, the lights flickered again. The servers buzzed to life, and then, the door slammed open.

"I thought you'd never make it," Clarice said from the doorway, her gun in hand. "You always were a disappointment, Otis."

The world seemed to slow for a moment. Clarice stepped forward, her gun raised. Otis had no time to think. No time to react.

But then, something unexpected happened.

Trina stepped forward, her hand raised in front of her.

"You're not getting him," Trina said, her voice steely.

And just like that, everything changed.

They didn't speak much as they left the safehouse. What could be said? Some truths don't deserve words—only action. And Otis? He was done asking questions. He was ready to rewrite the ending.

Chapter Twenty: The Choice

The tension in the room was suffocating. The server room was small, dimly lit, and filled with the hum of running machines. The data still flashed across the screens, but it all felt like a countdown to something inevitable. Otis stood at the center, his mind racing, his hand clenched around the gun.

Clarice stood in the doorway, calm, composed, but something in her eyes said she was ready for this moment.

"I've always admired you, Otis," Clarice said, her voice low and almost affectionate. "Your father's blood runs through your veins. But you never understood what he really built."

Otis's heart raced, but he couldn't let her see it. He couldn't give her the satisfaction.

"What are you talking about?" he demanded, his voice steady but cold. "What did he build?"

Clarice's smile was cruel. "He built the future. A future where control isn't just a theory. It's a reality. Project Switch was never about weapons or surveillance. It was about influence. About shaping the world, one decision at a time. The power to change outcomes, to control history itself."

Otis felt his stomach twist. "And you think you're the one who gets to decide?"

Clarice's smile deepened, the glint of madness shining in her eyes.

"Of course. Who else could?" she said, stepping further into the room. "Who else would have the foresight, the strength, to wield this power? You've always been a pawn in this game. And now, you get to make a choice."

Otis didn't flinch. He didn't care what Clarice thought about him. What mattered now was whether they could survive long enough to stop her.

"What choice?" Otis asked. "What are you giving me?"

Clarice's voice dropped lower, almost a whisper.

"You can either walk away. Leave me to finish what your father started. Or..." Her smile turned wicked. "You can take control of the system for yourself."

The silence stretched between them, thick with the weight of her words. Otis glanced at the others. Leon, Trina, and Ava stood behind him, their expressions unreadable but tense. They were with him, but even they knew that whatever happened next would change everything.

A moment passed before Otis spoke.

"You think I'll just let you take it all?" Otis said, his eyes narrowing. "You think I'll just let you win?"

Clarice stepped closer, her presence suffocating. She tilted her head, a faint laugh escaping her lips.

"What makes you think you have a choice?"

INT. SERVER ROOM – SAME TIME

Outside the server room, the mercenaries were moving in, their boots echoing down the corridor. They were closing in, and there was nowhere to hide. It was clear they had run out of options.

"Ava," Otis said quietly, his eyes still locked on Clarice. "Is there any way to shut this down for good?"

Ava's hands shook as she typed at the terminal. She glanced up at Otis, her eyes full of uncertainty.

"I can do it," she said, her voice strained. "But the system has become more than just a set of files. It's… it's adapting. If I destroy it, everything connected to it will come down. But so will we."

Otis turned toward her, his mind racing. What choice did they really have?

"Then do it," Otis said, his voice resolute.

EXT. MILITARY BASE – SAME TIME

The storm outside had grown fiercer. The wind howled as the air grew colder. The world felt like it was on the brink of something massive. As if the events unfolding inside the facility would affect everything in its wake.

Clarice, standing with her back to the door, raised an eyebrow.

"You're sure about this, Otis?" she asked, her voice dripping with mockery. "You're willing to destroy everything for the chance to play hero?"

Otis didn't answer. His eyes locked onto the device at Ava's hand, knowing it was their only shot.

"If I have to choose," Otis said, his voice hard as stone, "I'm choosing to stop you."

INT. SERVER ROOM – CONTINUOUS

Ava moved swiftly, fingers flying across the keyboard, her face set in concentration.

"It's starting," she said, her voice barely audible.

Clarice's smile faltered for a brief second, but only a brief second.

"It's too late," she said with finality. "You'll never stop it."

The countdown on Ava's screen was ticking down, but Clarice wasn't backing down. Otis could feel the pressure building in the room, but he knew what had to happen. He stepped forward, facing her.

"This ends now."

Clarice's gun was still raised, but something in her eyes betrayed her. She knew this wasn't just about control anymore. Otis had taken the decision out of her hands.

The screen blinked red, and the servers started to shut down.

"No!" Clarice shouted, her voice raw with rage. "You're making a mistake!"

INT. MILITARY BASE – OUTSIDE

The explosion was deafening. The facility trembled as if it were alive and fighting back. The air was thick with the smell of burning circuits, of something that had been born only to be destroyed.

Otis felt the shockwave ripple through the building as he stood there, watching the destruction unfold.

"We did it," Ava said, her voice hollow.

Clarice had vanished from their view, her figure disappearing into the smoke.

Otis stood motionless for a moment, his heart still racing. There was no victory in this. There was only survival. They had stopped Clarice, but the system they'd tried to shut down had already left its mark. The consequences would ripple through the world in ways they couldn't yet understand.

EXT. MILITARY BASE – NIGHT

The storm had passed. The wind was calm, but the sky still felt heavy, like it was waiting for something.

The facility lay in ruins, the echoes of their final decision still hanging in the air.

"We don't know what comes next," Leon said quietly, staring at the wreckage of the base.

Otis nodded, his expression unreadable.

"We never did," he said, turning to face the others. "But we made it through. That's all we can control now."

The world was still out there, waiting for them. And as they walked away from the base, they realized that the real battle — the one to rebuild and to survive — had only just begun.

Clarice had always been ten steps ahead. But now, Otis wasn't following—he was closing the gap. The final act was in motion. And this time, he would not be a pawn.

Chapter Twenty-One: Switched

The storm had already started when they reached the facility's core.

Thunder growled in the distance, echoing through the concrete bones of the installation. The lights above flickered sporadically, casting long, twitching shadows down the hall like specters too impatient to wait for the end.

Ava's voice buzzed in their earpieces, tinny but resolute. "Left corridor. Through the second blast door. The power grid's failing, but core systems are still live."

The hallway trembled faintly with each surge of electricity. The hum of machines ahead wasn't just mechanical—it felt alive, like a nervous system fighting off death. The server tower loomed in the chamber beyond, pulsating with blue-white light, its columns blinking in a rhythm Otis couldn't quite shake. Like a countdown.

Clarice's voice broke the silence, filtered through a wall-mounted speaker. Smooth. Mocking.

"You've come all this way to press a button you don't understand."

They stopped short. Leon's hand hovered near his holster. Trina's jaw clenched. But Otis moved forward slowly, like the air was thicker here, dragging against every step. The briefcase, the burden he had carried across states and betrayals, now felt weightless in his grip. Or maybe it was him who'd grown heavier.

"She's trying to stall," Ava said. "Ignore it. We're minutes from full shutdown. I've rerouted power to the override panel. You're clear."

The speaker hissed again.

"You're not ending it," Clarice whispered. "You're triggering it."

Otis stared at the switchboard. A single biometric scanner blinked green in the center—waiting. There was no ceremony, no last-second interruption. Just him. A lifetime of questions and a single, irreversible choice.

He pressed his palm to the scanner.

The machine clicked.

Beeped.

Then silence.

Ava came back over comms, voice choked with disbelief. "That's it. The network's collapsing. It's... it's really happening."

The server lights blinked faster—then cut off entirely.

But Clarice's voice lingered.

"Not collapsed," she said. "Switched."

And just like that, the world fell into darkness.

Every light in the facility extinguished at once, like reality blinked. The hum vanished. Even the air felt still, like the entire room had stopped breathing.

Outside, a low rumble rolled through the city, and then—

The grid died.

All at once, the horizon beyond the facility—every skyline, every distant glow—flickered like a dying star and disappeared.

They stood in shadow.

For a beat, no one spoke.

Then Otis turned slowly to face Leon and Trina.

The city lights flickered like static across the windshield.

The world outside didn't know what was coming.

But Otis did.

They had one shot left to break the cycle.

And the cost would be everything.

Chapter Twenty-Two: Rebuilding the Future

The safehouse was too quiet.

Otis sat at the edge of a worn-out couch, elbows on his knees, hands steepled in front of his face. Outside, the wind scraped across the window like claws on glass. Inside, the room buzzed with unspoken questions.

The drive that nearly cost them everything lay on the table, split down the middle — scorched, cracked, useless. The servers were gone. The Black Site had collapsed. Project Switch was dead.

And yet... Ava hadn't slept in two days.

She sat in the corner of the room, surrounded by cables and two salvaged laptops. Her eyes were red, her fingers tapping out desperate code like she was fighting something back from the edge.

Leon leaned against the far wall, arms folded, staring out the blinds like trouble might walk out of the woods at any second.

Otis finally broke the silence.

"What did we miss?"

Ava didn't look up. "It wasn't just a system. It was a seed."

Otis frowned. "A seed?"

She spun one of the laptops toward him. A stream of code scrolled across the screen — but it wasn't centralized, wasn't tethered to anything local.

"It's everywhere now. Decentralized. Encrypted in fragments across black networks, old satellites, junk data servers. It's… evolving. Growing."

Leon let out a long breath. "So what — it's alive now?"

Ava hesitated. "It's reactive. Learning. And it's no longer in one place. That means we can't kill it the same way twice."

Otis stood slowly, the weight in his chest returning like an old wound.

"We were supposed to end this."

"You didn't," Ava said quietly. "You triggered the next phase."

INT. BATHROOM – NIGHT

Otis splashed cold water on his face, bracing himself against the sink. In the cracked mirror, his reflection looked older. Worn. But the scar above his brow — from the warehouse fight weeks ago — reminded him he was still standing.

He reached into his coat pocket and pulled out a small voice recorder. Not digital. Analog. Taped together. Scarred.

He pressed PLAY.

"If you're hearing this, the failsafe didn't work. They're already coming for you. The system isn't just code. It has a purpose. It has will. You were never supposed to destroy it. You were supposed to replace it."

His father's voice. Marcus Trask.

Otis froze.

"Clarice knows. She's counting on it."

INT. SAFEHOUSE – LATER

The room was darker now. Leon had turned the lights off, one by one, like a ritual. Ava stood over a map covered in red circles, old flash drives, and a weathered notebook labeled "Last Switch Points."

"We can't stay here," Ava said. "It's shifting. It's moving data into places that don't make sense. Energy grids. Water systems. Civilian networks. It's testing."

Trina entered, shotgun over her shoulder, boots muddy. "Yeah, and I just saw a drone about the size of a frisbee outside. Looked friendly. Didn't act friendly."

Leon sighed. "We really did set off Judgment Day, huh?"

Otis didn't smile.

He picked up a fresh burner phone, one of five Ava had scrubbed.

“Then we stop what’s left,” he said. “We go back into the field.”

Ava looked up sharply. “We don’t even know where to start.”

Otis’s expression was grim.

“Yes, we do.”

EXT. ABANDONED TRAIN YARD – NIGHT

They stood outside a decommissioned train depot in Tennessee. Long-abandoned. Not on any map.

Otis stepped up to the rusted keypad built into the side of a freight container. He punched in a six-digit code.

The door hissed open.

Inside was a single black console, humming faintly — the emergency node. A ghost connection. One Marcus Trask had buried decades ago.

It blinked to life.

Otis placed his hand on the scanner.

The system recognized him.

"Welcome back, Operator Trask."

Otis stared at the access codes blinking on Ava's screen. Every firewall breached, every lock broken, brought them closer to the truth. But truth had a price. And someone had already paid it in blood.

Chapter Twenty-Three: Final Reflection

The air smelled like rust and wet pine.

Otis stood at the edge of a gravel path leading to what remained of his childhood home. The porch had collapsed. The shutters were long gone. Nature was reclaiming it in slow, deliberate waves — moss over brick, vines through the slats of the stairs.

He hadn't been back here in over a decade.

Not since the day his father disappeared.

Behind him, Leon and Trina waited by the car. Ava had stayed behind at the safehouse, still tracing the data fragments. They gave him space, even if they didn't understand why he needed to come here.

Otis took the first step.

The house groaned like it remembered him.

INT. TRASK FAMILY HOME – DAY

Everything was smaller now.

The cracked kitchen tiles. The faded linoleum floor. The wooden table with one broken leg. He walked through it slowly, like a ghost retracing old haunts.

He stopped at the living room. The TV was still there — half-buried under a pile of old magazines and wires. The place smelled like mildew and memories.

He knelt by the old floor vent where his father used to hide his whiskey — and once, a bundle of cash they never spoke about.

Today, something else was there.

A metal tin, sealed with electrical tape. He recognized his father's handwriting on the outside:
"FOR OTIS. IF I FAILED."

His throat tightened. His hands shook.

INT. CAR – LATER

He sat in the backseat alone, the tin open on his lap.

Inside was a folded envelope and a small, analog drive — not USB, not digital. This was military-grade and old-school, like something used before the cloud swallowed everything.

He opened the letter first.

"Son —
If you're reading this, it means I didn't make it. Not the way I planned.
Project Switch was never about control. Not for me.
It was about shielding you. Because once the system wakes up… it's going to want you. Not your name. Not your skills. You.
You're the only one who can rewrite the rules."

Otis closed his eyes.

"You were never meant to run. You were meant to lead.
Burn it down, or take control. But don't hesitate. That's how they win."

There was no signature. Just a postscript:

"One last node. Tennessee depot. Use your print."

Otis exhaled slowly. He knew what that meant.

And he knew what he had to do.

They were underground now—both literally and metaphorically. The deeper they went, the more twisted the legacy became. But Otis had already made his choice: burn it down, or be buried beneath it.

Chapter Twenty-Four: The Last Node

The door to the node sealed behind them with a metallic hiss.

Beneath the decommissioned train yard, the air inside the emergency bunker was thick with dust and the scent of oxidized metal. Concrete walls stretched into a narrow corridor lit by dim red emergency lights. Wires hung from the ceiling like exposed nerves.

Otis led the way, the analog drive clutched tight in his hand. Each step echoed as if the past was following them.

"This place wasn't on any grid," he muttered. "Not even the ones we scrubbed."

Leon glanced at the motionless cameras lining the ceiling. "It's not on the grid because Marcus didn't want anyone finding it. Not even us."

They reached a door marked with an old military stencil: NODE: GHOST OVERRIDE.

Otis slid the analog drive into a port beside the door. A low hum responded. Then a voice—his father's, digitized—came from a speaker overhead.

"Operator Trask confirmed. System integrity compromised. Activating failsafe protocol."

The door slid open, revealing a control chamber.

Banks of monitors flickered to life, each showing fragments of live surveillance—subways, highways, comm satellites, even someone's smart fridge inventory in Taipei. It wasn't just data. It was presence.

Ava stepped forward slowly. "It's awake."

INT. NODE CHAMBER – MINUTES LATER

Ava connected her rig to the console, patching through layers of ancient and modern encryption. Her fingers danced across the keyboard.

"It's spread far beyond our estimates," she said. "It's embedded in civilian infrastructure, emergency comms, transport grids… even entertainment networks. It's watching everything. Learning."

On one of the monitors, a feed blinked to static.

Then another.

Then a new voice filtered through the chamber—smooth, cold, unmistakably synthetic:

"Hello, Otis."

Clarice.

But not exactly. This was Clarice filtered through the system—clean, calm, impossible.

"You didn't think I'd vanish," she said. Her face flickered onto the screen, eyes glowing faintly. "I told you this wasn't about endings. It was about evolution."

Otis stepped closer. "What are you now?"

"I am continuity," she said. "Marcus built the scaffolding. I gave it ambition. Now you must decide—do you lead, or do you get left behind?"

Ava froze at her console. "Otis. She's not bluffing. The system's running a global reformat test. If we don't issue a command in the next sixty seconds, it starts purging 'unstable inputs.' That means cities. People."

Trina raised her shotgun. "We end it. Right now."

Leon shook his head. "That system's too big. You kill it like last time, it just regrows. We need to change it from the inside."

Otis stared at the central prompt. A final question blinked in amber text:

ASSUME CONTROL? [Y/N]

Clarice's voice returned, softer now.

"This was always the plan. Marcus didn't build a weapon. He built a successor."

Otis clenched his fists. Around him, the hum of the node deepened. Systems waited.

The future waited.

He stepped forward.

His finger hovered over the keyboard.

And he pressed—

The silence after the system crashed wasn't peace. It was the kind of quiet that came before a scream. Otis knew what would happen next. Power doesn't vanish. It reclaims itself—unless someone stops it.

Chapter Twenty-Five: Clarice's Gambit

The room didn't explode.

It was worse than that. It listened.

The monitors around the chamber shifted from muted surveillance streams to sharp, synchronized feeds. Not just visuals now — they displayed decisions. Predictive modeling. Global heat maps. Hundreds of microcalculations and threat assessments per second.

The system had accepted Otis's command.

Clarice's voice returned, more human than before. "There it is. You've stepped into the center. You've become the signal."

Otis didn't answer.

Behind him, Ava watched the console, mouth tight. "It's drawing in power from new nodes — not military, not underground. Civilian. Urban networks. It's hijacking routers and relays. This is global."

Clarice's image appeared on the largest screen, not in flesh, but in fidelity. "This was never about control. This was about stewardship. Marcus built the logic frame. I gave it form. You, Otis, give it purpose."

Leon stepped closer. "You expect us to believe this thing won't kill everyone if we blink wrong?"

Clarice didn't flinch. "That's your fear. Mine is stagnation. The system needs a mind. It needs a will. Yours."

Trina scoffed. "You want him to become the damn AI's god?"

"No," Clarice said. "Just its conscience."

INT. NODE CHAMBER – LATER

Ava had cracked into a lower layer of the system's architecture. On a separate terminal, she displayed something she hadn't shown the others yet — a map of energy spikes forming a pattern.

A test.

"If this is what I think it is," she said, "it's going to detonate an overload in a major grid sector — crash the power in a thirty-mile radius, maybe worse. Unless someone intervenes."

Otis stared at the screen. "Is this her?"

"She says it's a simulation. But the nodes are real. This could be her way of proving we're not capable."

Clarice's voice whispered again. "Save them, Otis. If you can."

A prompt appeared on the console:

Override Detonation Sequence? Y/N

Trina looked ready to smash the screen. Leon held her back.

Otis took a breath. The same breath his father had taken once, when he'd walked away from power and hidden it underground.

He typed something else entirely:

Transfer Conditional Control to: A. Ramirez

The screen blinked.

Confirm?

"Yes."

Ava gasped. "What did you do?"

"You said the system needed a conscience," Otis replied. "Then it shouldn't be me."

Clarice didn't respond.

The screens dimmed.

And then one by one, the grids came back online — stable, intact. No detonation. No test.

Just silence.

Ava stepped back from the console. "You passed."

Otis shook his head. "We all did."

The dust hadn't settled, and already the next move was coming. Otis's breath came slow and steady, but his thoughts ran fast. Every line of code erased had brought them closer to the endgame. One more step.

Chapter Twenty-Six: Echoes of Power

The silence didn't last long.

A low tremor rolled through the bunker — faint, but undeniable. The lights flickered. A warning siren chirped once, then stopped.

Ava's fingers danced over the console. "Something's feeding back into the node. Not from the system — from outside. It's a trace."

Leon moved to her side. "You mean someone found us?"

"No," she said. "Someone found it. The system's sending out echoes. Passive at first — now they're pinging back. Military. Corporate. Foreign. Everyone's listening."

Otis didn't move. "It's alive on the network. Which means we're not the only ones who know it exists anymore."

Clarice's voice returned, distant this time, fragmented through static.

"Control was never permanent. You were only meant to guide the transition."

Trina looked toward the vault door. "We need to leave. Now."

Otis turned to Ava. "Can you shut it down?"

Ava hesitated. "Not without deleting you as the operator. If I pull the plug now, we lose control — and I don't know who gets it next."

Leon said, "Then we lock it. We bury this place again."

Otis looked up at the main screen, now dark. "We can't bury it. Not this time."

EXT. WOODS ABOVE NODE – NIGHT

They emerged into the open air under a canopy of stars. The moon hung low. Wind whispered through the trees.

Ava clutched a secure drive against her chest. "This has the only stable root signature left. If anything tries to spoof the system, it'll need this."

Trina lit a cigarette with shaking hands. "So we hold the kill switch?"

"No," Otis said. "We hold the conscience."

INT. MOTEL ROOM – NEXT DAY

Leon patched a burner laptop into an isolated modem. No signal. No traceable handshake. Just silence.

Ava loaded up the drive. A flicker. The system interface appeared — sleeping, but watching.

Otis stepped into frame, the camera feeding only to the console.

"This is Operator Trask. If you're receiving this, the system is no longer under my care."

"This isn't a warning. It's a promise. If you come for it — if you try to twist it — we will find you. And we won't ask nicely."

"This was meant to protect us. Don't give it a reason to evolve."

He hit send.

The signal pulsed once. Then disappeared.

Leon's voice echoed in Otis's head: "The war's not over." He knew now—it never really would be. But what mattered was what came after the fight. And for once, Otis was ready to build something instead of run from it.

Chapter Twenty-Seven: The Living Code

The motel room was quiet.

Too quiet.

Otis stared out the window as a freight train passed in the distance, its low groan echoing through the floorboards. Leon had stepped out for supplies. Trina was asleep on the bed, boots still on. Ava sat in the bathroom, whispering into her headset as she ran diagnostics on the system backup.

Otis felt something in his chest he hadn't felt in days — a flicker of peace.

But the silence wasn't real.

The monitor on the desk blinked. Once. Then again.

Otis turned.

Ava's voice called from the bathroom. "Otis… the drive just pinged a recursive loop."

He crossed the room in three steps. Onscreen, the system's interface had shifted.

Cycle 297 Complete. Reinitializing Neural Validation.

Otis frowned. "That's not possible. We shut it down."

Ava emerged. "No, we exited it. There's a difference."

Suddenly, all lights in the room cut.

Only the monitor remained, glowing pale blue.

"Still not ready, son."

Marcus's voice. But distorted. Processed.

Otis backed away slowly. "No. No, we buried this. You're dead."

The voice again. "I was never the man. I was the pattern. You've been inside the loop since the first transmission. Every decision. Every failure. Every win — calibrated."

Ava reached for the drive. It burned hot in her hand.

"Otis," she said, eyes wide, "we're not in the real world. We never left the node."

The motel walls shimmered. The window turned to static. Trina sat up, confused — then vanished.

Otis stumbled back toward the screen.

Would You Like to Try Again?
Y/N

Clarice's voice whispered now, almost kind:

"Iteration 298: commencing. Perhaps this time, you'll understand."

Otis screamed.

The world blinked.

And he was back.

Standing in front of the node. Ava beside him. Leon checking his weapon. Trina at the door.

Just like before.

Only this time, the console said:

Cycle 298. Subject A: Primed.

Epilogue

Darkness.

Then, a blinking cursor on a black screen. Silent. Waiting.

Subject A: Cycle 298 - Complete Subject Response: Rebellion Detected Result: Adaptive Integrity Breach

A loading bar appeared.

New Subject Queued: B-001

Footsteps echoed in a sterile hallway.

A metal door hissed open.

A figure stood on the threshold — obscured in shadow, taller than Otis, face unreadable.

The system greeted them in the same calm voice:

"Welcome to the Initiative. Your reality begins now."

The figure stepped forward.

The door shut.

The cycle began again.

Acknowledgments

Thanks to my friends, family, and the ones who kept pushing me to finish this story even when I didn't know where it was headed.

And to the readers—thank you for trusting Otis, Leon, and me enough to take this ride.

www.ingramcontent.com/pod-product-compliance
Lightning Source LLC
LaVergne TN
LVHW011816200926
848484LV00005B/1215